BY KAITLYN SIU AND MARCELO BADARI

First published in Great Britain in 2022
by Wayland
Copyright © Hodder and Stoughton, 2022

Editors: Elise Short and Grace Glendinning
Cover design: Peter Scoulding
Inside design: Emma DeBanks

HB ISBN: 978 1 5263 1579 3
PB ISBN: 978 1 5263 1580 9

Printed and bound in China

Wayland, an imprint of
Hachette Children's Group
Part of Hodder and Stoughton
Carmelite House
50 Victoria Embankment
London EC4Y 0DZ

An Hachette UK Company
www.hachette.co.uk
www.hachettechildrens.co.uk

MIX
Paper from
responsible sources
FSC® C104740
FSC
www.fsc.org

The website addresses (URLs) included in this book were valid at the time of
going to press. However, it is possible that contents or addresses may have
changed since the publication of this book. No responsibility for any such
changes can be accepted by either the author or the Publisher.

WHAT'S A VARIABLE?

Let's find out! It's story time at the library and you're invited to join super-reading-robot Flex as he writes a book all by himself. We'll have loads of fun and learn some cool coding facts. Let's get reading, super coders!

Flex is a super-robot who loves to read. With his amazing robot brain, he can read really fast. One day, he read a hundred books in one hour!

Flex especially loves
to visit the library.

Today Flex is heading out on his weekly trip to the library. He can't wait to find new books to read.

When Flex arrives at the library, he can't believe his good luck! The librarian tells him that they are running a special class on how to write books.

TODAY'S STORY TIME: WRITE YOUR OWN BOOK!

Flex is excited to learn how to write his own book.

He meets the story time teacher, Type, who tells Flex that he will learn to write a book called *All About Me* using a special **computer programming** game.

Computers can help us to write simple books!

All About Me

Type shows Flex the computer program that will help him with his book.

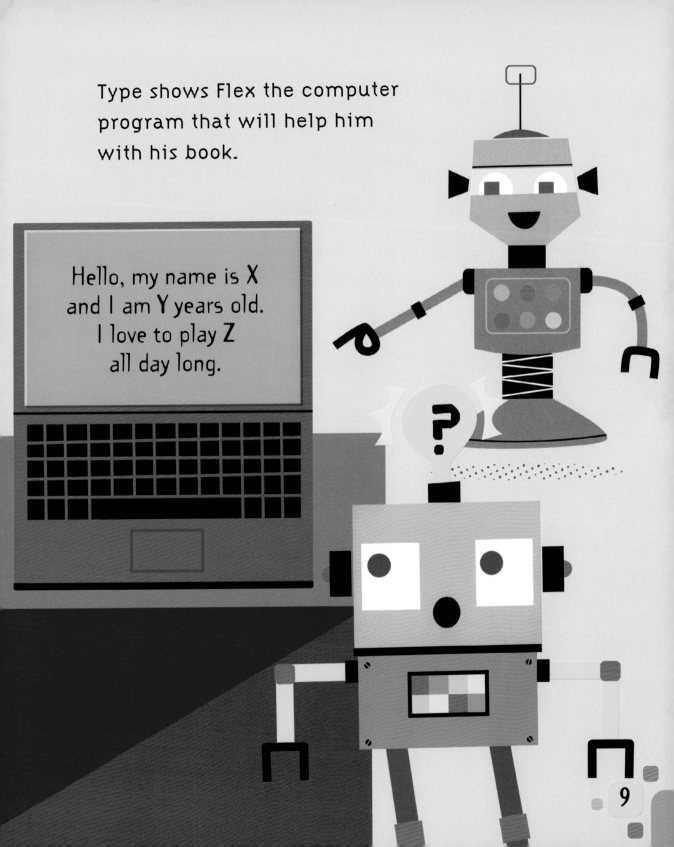

Hello, my name is **X** and I am **Y** years old. I love to play **Z** all day long.

That sounds very strange! What are the X, Y and Z for?

Hello, my name is **X** and I am **Y** years old. I love to play **Z** all day long.

Those are awesome bits of code called **variables!**

11

A variable is like a box that keeps information inside it.

It is a way of holding this information all together. Variables can hold all kinds of things, such as numbers, letters, words – whatever we want!

Variable

Variable

Variable

Variables are very important for computers. These little boxes help computer programs to **access** lots of information quickly and to make changes quickly, too.

All that amazing information inside each variable is called a **value**.

Flex, you will write your very own program to tell the computer what value the variables should have in your book! Like this:

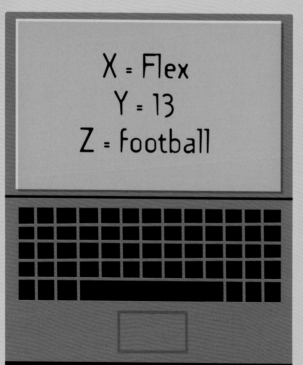

X = Flex
Y = 13
Z = football

Now the computer will **replace**
the variables with these values,
and the book will read:

Hello,
my name is **Flex**
and I am
13 years old.
I love to play
football all day long.

Flex looks at the next page of the book in the programming game. The code says:

X can't wait for the big Z tournament. He only has P sleeps left!

Flex plans values for these new variables and writes the program:

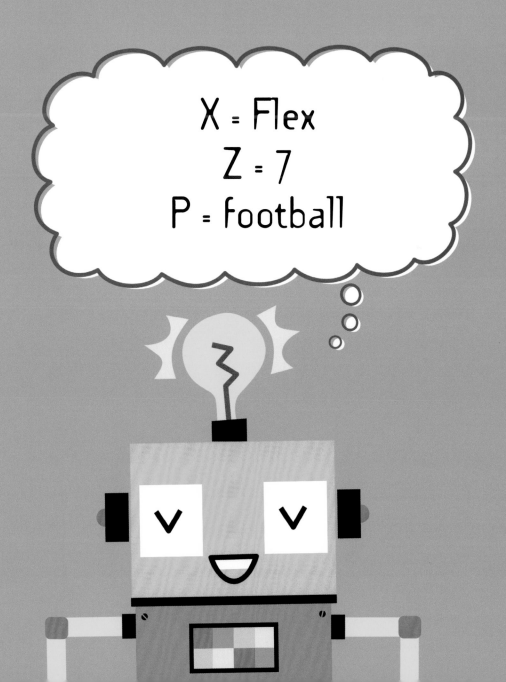

X = Flex
Z = 7
P = football

His book now reads:

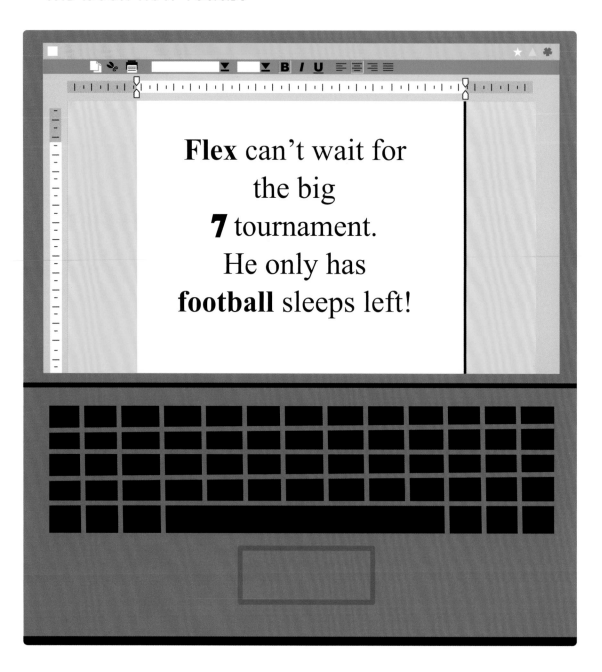

Flex can't wait for the big **7** tournament. He only has **football** sleeps left!

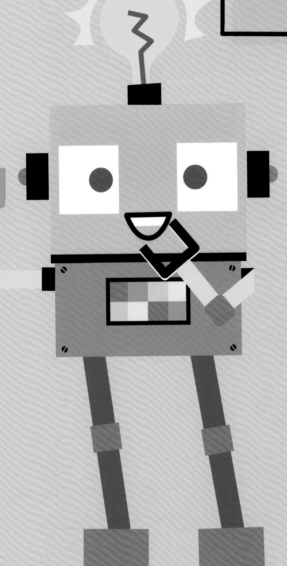

Oh no! There's a **bug** in the code!

No, not a real bug! It's a computer bug. You have to fix it, Flex. **Debug** that code!

Flex quickly sees that he mixed up
the values for the Z and P variables.

No worries! Flex simply tells the
computer the right values.

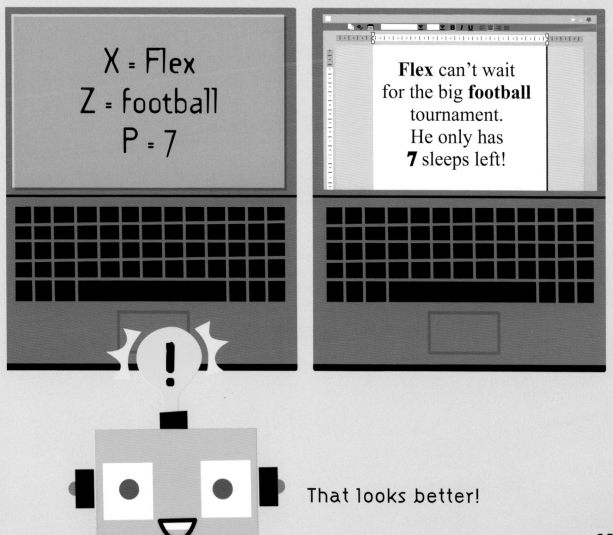

X = Flex
Z = football
P = 7

Flex can't wait
for the big **football**
tournament.
He only has
7 sleeps left!

That looks better!

Flex's friend Volt joins him at the
library. Volt loves Flex's story!

I would love to be
a character in a book!

Flex knows how to change his book quickly. He changes the value for the X variable in his code.

X = Volt

The book changes before his eyes and Volt's name appears in place of Flex's!

Hello, my name is **Volt** and I am **13** years old. I love to play **football** all day long.

Volt can't wait for the big **football** tournament. He only has **7** sleeps left!

Wow! Changing words is easy when you use variables.

Flex's book is complete! The librarian lets him print out one copy for Volt and one for himself.

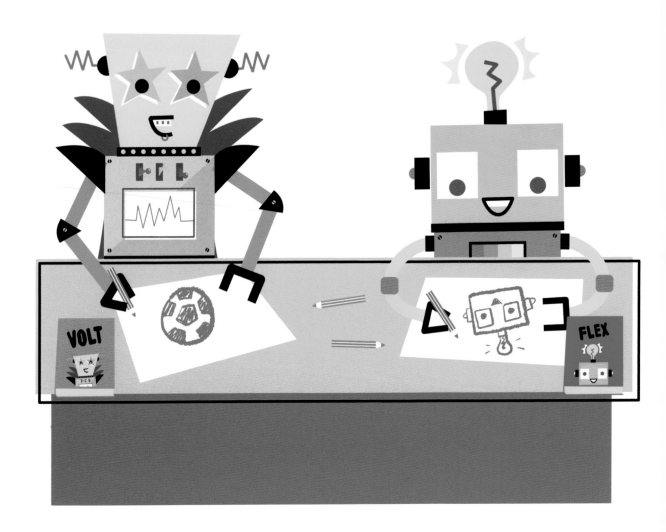

Flex and Volt each draw pictures to go with the words.

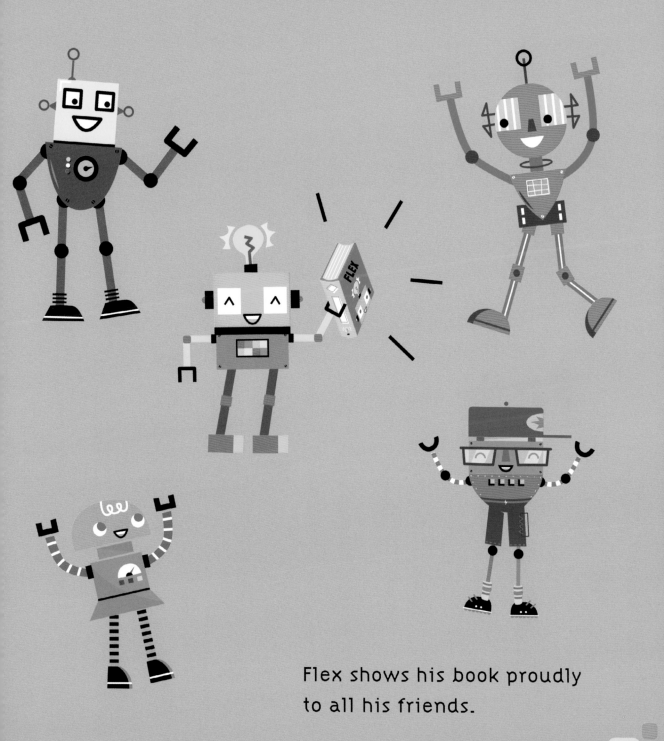

Flex shows his book proudly to all his friends.

Now it's your turn! It's time to write your own story. Choose values for your variables and read out your story.

Last year, I went on a **Y** trip to **X**. It was so much fun to see **Z** and **B**. **X** is a great place to visit with **P**. My favourite part of the trip was **U**.

Now for some bonus fun! Did you know that super coders can call the variables in their code whatever they want? If you don't like X, Y and Z, you can also name them something really simple, such as:

name = Flex
age = 13
activity = football

Of course, you can also name your variables something super silly!

Like silly banana? Funky monkey? Dancing dragon? Even happy hippo?

Can you think of any more hilarious variable names to use in your code?

Coding is great fun when you get creative!

GLOSSARY

Access: to get at, or be able to use something

Bug: a problem or error in coding instructions

Computer programming: writing the coding instructions that control a computer

Debug: find and solve a problem in coding instructions

Instruction: information that tells us what to do

Replace: to fill a spot with something new or different

Value: a type of information, such as a letter, number or word

Variable: a special box used in computer programming to store a value

GUIDE FOR TEACHERS, PARENTS AND CARERS

Young children can learn the basic concepts of coding. These concepts are the foundation of computer science, as well as other important skills, such as critical thinking and problem solving.

Variables in coding are like containers that store information. Variables help computers store a lot of information and access it quickly when running a program.

In this book, readers learn all about how variables can be used. We use the concept of writing a short book to learn the concept of assigning values to variables.

If you are looking for supplementary fun, consider this variables activity:

https://teachyourkidscode.com/variables-coding

INDEX